Photography Guidebook

Discover true photographer within you

AMARPREET SINGH

Publisher - The Thought Flame

THE THOUGHT FLAME

TURNING SPARK INTO FLAME

info@thethoughtflame.com

www.thethoughtflame.com

Table of Contents

Introduction

Let me ask you two questions: how many pictures do you currently have hanging in your house and how many pictures do you take on a day-to-day basis? If you have more than four pictures hanging around your home or take more than two pictures a day, you may have the heart of a true photographer.

Let's face it, without photos in our lives our world would pretty much be meaningless. Pictures today are more than capturing a moment between two people, recording the life of a child or even sharing a special moment between a couple of friends. Photos have been used since the camera was first invented people have been recording important moments throughout history such as World War I to the horrific events of 9/11.

Photos in general not only allow us to capture the most important moments in our lives and to hold them close to our hearts, but they capture the most important events throughout our history so that in the future the people living in that era can see and experience what kind of world we lived in.

Becoming a photographer is far from easy. There are many different things that you need to learn about before you can just pick up a professional camera and began capturing as many pictures as you want. You need to learn about every part of the camera so you understand how and when it is used, the difference between certain lenses and the difference between the different shooting modes available.

That is when this eBook steps in. I can teach you everything that you need to know about photography down to the very basics so that you can begin taking breath taking photos and perhaps even make a living off of it.

Chapter One: Why You Should Become A Photographer and The Importance of Photography

Whether you accept it or not, our memories will eventually fade. That is just the reality, however there are a variety of ways that we can hold onto our precious memories and that is through the use of many photographs that we hang in our homes. Unlike photos our memories of certain important events or moments in our lives become fuzzy over time and eventually we end up forgetting where and when those important moments occurred. No matter how hard you try you will never remember the exact details of those events as you grow older.

Photos on the other hand give us the opportunity to archive our most important memories not only in our delicate minds, but also in our homes. These photos allow us to share our precious memories with the people will love such as friends and family and also gives us the chance to share our memories with future generations to come.

There is always that one person within our family that is excellent as documentary the most important memories and events that occur throughout our lives. For me that person is my father and rare is the day that you don't see him with his trusty professional camera. When I was younger I remember complaining to my dad that he took too many pictures and that I didn't want to stand in any of them. Of course in the end my father won all of these arguments and today I'm glad that he did. He often takes out the old family photo album from time to time and shows off the photos and sometimes I come across one that I do not recognize the scenery or the person within it. The stories that come along with these photos simply amaze me and I love the fact that yes one picture is worth more than a thousand words. As you can imagine today I stand willingly for these photos and more often than not ask to receive a double of all of them as well.

Our own family photos are not the only pictures that are important to us. Pictures that document important events in history are as equally important. The people behind the most distinguishable photos that we know of today such as those depicting the events of World War II, 9/11 or even the Columbine shooting tragedy are able to freeze the most terrifying moments in such a way that video is unable to do it justice. These photos not only help us to remember those important moments, but they also help us to reflect on the sadness and disturbing aspect of those events and cause us to reflect on our own lives. Take the earthquake that hit Japan as an example. When you see pictures of this day and how they show people running from their homes in terror or see how the tsunami swept away everything in its path, you can help but think of how frail our lives really are. Photos like these are important because our memory of the events will only go so far and our memories will not remain whole for long.

Photography in general plays an extremely crucial role in both our history and in our future. Whether a person is the family documentarian, a photographic journalist or even war documentarians, all of these people have what is perhaps the most important job in the world. Their main duty in life is to take a record of these events and to archive them so that future generations can learn from those events. These pictures are even especially important in today's world with the use of Twitter, Facebook and even YouTube as photos can be easily passed around for people all over the world to see. Pictures distributed on these social platforms are able to pass around the world in a matter of minutes and can be seen by anybody who owns a computer, laptop or tablet.

Photos are also important because they help to archive the special images or memories that you want to remember over time. These pictures can be anything from your child's first birthday to a tornado hitting your home. Regardless of what it may be you can take a variety of pictures to share with your family or your friends or whoever you wish. Having these pictures available can help you to explain any kind of story better as you can show people exactly what it is you are talking about, even if you don't remember that well yourself.

The Difference between Whether Your Should Become A Photographer and If You Could Become A Photographer

Before you can even think about becoming a photographer, it is important to figure out the difference between choosing photography as something you will thoroughly enjoy or as a full time profession. It is important because becoming a professional photographer is something that may sound amazing, but that involves a lot of surprisingly hard work. For example, I love to cook for people and cook as often as I can during the week, but that doesn't mean that I want to open my own restaurant. If I were to open my own restaurant I would probably end up doing most of the things that I would hate doing in the first place such as scrubbing dishes, inventory or even payroll. I would rather spend my time cooking the dishes I love rather than doing all of that.

The same thing goes for photography. There is more to it than just taking a few pictures and I'm sure that once you learn every aspect of photography you may want to think about choosing another profession. In this section we will outline everything that you need to know about the subject of photography and I will give you some insight on what professional photography is all about.

The first thing that we need to do is define exactly what professional photography is. What this pretty much means is that you earn a decent income taking pictures of people or events. What you need to understand that the money you make has nothing to do with what kind of skills you have. You don't have to go to school and spend a ton of money to learn how to take pictures. You just take a picture, that is it.

In order to become a professional photographer the first thing that you need to do is to start your own photography business. Of course you don't have to open your own business that is the best way to start earning a decent income. While this may seem like an easy feat, that is necessarily not the case. There are a variety of things that you must consider first before you have the chance to earn money off of your photos.

1. Identify Your General Market-you need to sit down and ask yourself who is going to pay you for your photos and why they would even consider buying your photos. You can target newlywed couples to first time parents.

2. Need to Get Out and Prospect Potential Clients-how are people going to find you if they have never heard of your or your business? You need to go out in public and spread the word around whether that is with business cards or setting up business meetings for families and companies.

3. Sell Yourself-in order to begin earning some good cash you will need to sell yourself and whatever photography skills you may have. People are not just going to hand over the money they have if they haven't seen what you are capable of. You need to sell them on your skills and show them with a portfolio of your work what you can do.

4. Deliver Your Work-when you are hired for a job or a project, it is important that you deliver your work on the date it has been agreed upon. Never miss a deadline and never not deliver your work.

5. Don't Forget To Market Your Work-in order for word to spread of your company and in order for you to earn some more money, you will need to market yourself and your work. There are a variety of ways that you can do this either by passing out flyers or taking to the internet and marketing yourself via social media channels.

6. Planning Ahead-In order to help your company grow you need to know where you want your company to be in the next five years. Plan ahead and try to invest in your future by starting a company website, buying the latest photography equipment or even buying a company car.

7. Know Your Legal Rights-in order to prevent yourself from getting sued in the future I highly recommend that you thoroughly research what kind of legal rights you have. Consult a lawyer whenever you are ready and have them walk you through your legal rights and what you should do in the event of a lawsuit.

8. Collect As Much Gear As Possible-investing on new equipment is all a part of the job and if you plan on being the best professional photographer that you can be I highly recommend that you invest in the latest equipment. While it may become pricey in the long run, these things are all necessary if you plan on your business growing in the future.

Now I know that you must be reading this and telling yourself, "That is a lot! No wonder everybody doesn't want to become a professional photographer." Now while you may understand what it truly takes to become a professional photographer, the next thing that you need to ask yourself is if you can do this. I wouldn't worry too much about that part just yet. I would concentrate on doing what you love most which is taking pictures. The best part about the thing that you love most is that you can be as creative as you want with your photos and you have the freedom to take whatever photos you want. Revel in that and keep taking pictures of the things you love.

How To Become A Great Photographer

Now that you understand whether or not professional photography is for you, the next thing that you need to learn is how you can become a great photographer. The first thing that you need to do in order to learn how to become a great photographer is to figure out for yourself what kind of photographer you want to become in the long run. There are many types of photographers such as documentarians and personal photographers. If you are like me then you may hate the idea of taking someone's picture without having their consent first. If that is the case then becoming a documentarian is not the route that you want to take. If you like the idea of spending some time with the subjects of your photos and like the idea of having your clients involved as much in the photo shoot as you are then I highly recommend becoming a professional photographers that specializes in weddings or family photos.

Photography is all about touching the lives and environment of the people and surroundings around you. It is all about making special connections and it enables all of us to bridges important gaps within culture, generations and even languages. Photography is a powerful thing and as such it is not meant to be taken lightly.

So, the question becomes what makes a great photographer? It does not come down to what kind of equipment they have or even what kind of images they capture. It all comes down to the overall character of the photographer rather than what they have. These kinds of photographers are people just like you and me and even you can become a great photographer. Here is a list of the different attributes you should have if you ever expect to become a great photographer that many people would love to hire to capture their special moment.

1. You Need To Have Some Kind of Humility-while I know that a photographer is someone who can hold up a camera, you need to keep in mind that there is more to it than that. While you and I have the ability to create breathtaking and beautiful photos, we have the potential to create bad ones as well. We are not better than anybody else and this is something that you need to keep in mind if you plan on succeeding as a photographer.

You need to keep in mind that in order to achieve any kind of special status in photographer you must learn the act of humility first. While you may "know" how to do something, you cannot let your ego dictate whether or not you ask for help if you need it.

There are many things that we as humans need help with and the first part of showing humility is accepting help whenever it is necessary. In order to become a great photographer, you must understand and be willing to ask for help if you are lacking in ability in a certain area.

In my many years of experience I have found that there are three different types of photographers out there. The first kind of photographer that you may come across is also known as a technical photographer. This person is all about what kind of equipment they should have and are experts as using formulas in order to generate results. This is the kind of photographer that can easily give you details on how many millimeters they plan to shoots and what kind of focal lengths they will need.

The next photographer that you may come across is also known as the subject photographer. This kind of photographer is known to study their subjects intensely and can tell you everything you need to know about the object. This photographer knows everything about his or her subject from its breeding habits to where it resides on a longitude and latitude scale.

The third kind of photographer that you may come across is what I like to call the artistic photographer. To this person does not care about what kind of photo they have just taken or how they managed to take a picture of it. The only thing that matters to this person is how the picture comes out and if it is the most beautiful thing they have ever managed to capture.

Each of these photographers plays an important role in the entire field of photography. However, each type of photographer lacks the necessary skills to fill in the role of another type of photographer. While the technical photographer is too busy spending time and money getting the latest equipment, they will never be able to fully understand the fundamentals of important composition. A subject photographer may become single-minded and remain focused on capturing their next image of the animal they are pursuing to concentrate on the fact that the people who are going to view their pictures are not going to understand the subject as intimately as they do. The creative photographer is too busy taking pictures of random objects that concentrating on why they are taking the picture in the first place.

2. You Need to Have Both Perseverance and Patience-one of the many important traits that every photographer needs to accept are both patience and perseverance. You need to have patience because not every great photo is just going to fall into your lap. There are going to be times when you are going to have to travel countless miles, wait countless hours and endure the worst weather you will ever encounter just to get that great picture. If you are the type of person who wants the kind of picture they want when they want it, you are going to be the photographer that will miss a lot of promising pictures.

A perfect example of this is when you photographing both children and animals. Let's face it, both animals and children never do the things that we want nor expect them to do and the same applies to taking pictures of them. They will never stay perfectly still in a certain pose nor will they full listen to your instructions. The whole of photographing both parties is to capture the precious moments when they are doing things that we less expect and it s make the picture even cuter because of it. Taking pictures of both children and animals requires a lot of patience on your part and without it you will surely miss taking those perfect cute pictures.

Having patience takes a lot of organization. When you are ready to take a picture make a list of the things you will need to have with you during your "photo shoot." If you are taking pictures of wildlife you need to know whether the animals are nocturnal or not so that you can be out in their domain at the time they are most active. You will then need to figure out what kind of light you are going to need to capture them at that particular time of the day. The next thing you need to remember is what kind of filters you are going to need and what other equipment you may find yourself needing in an emergency situation. If you are doing a photo shoot in a studio or office building, plan out the props and background you are going to be using. The key is to do various things in advance so that your photo shoot can go off without hitch.

When it comes to perseverance, this means that you may need to return to a certain area or location time and time again if you haven't captured the photo that you wanted. For example if the first set of photos you have taken are not as perfect as you want, you will need to remind yourself that is not what you wanted and you will need to plan on taking a second trip to capture the perfect pictures that you want. In my experience I have taken pictures of the same thing over and over again just to get the picture that I imagined taking beforehand. It happens to nearly every photographer so do not feel like a failure if you need to go out a second time. All you are doing is tweaking the overall photography process until you get the perfect shot.

3. Observation is Key-the way that you can become a great photographer in the long run is to develop your own special power of observation. The one thing that I highly recommend to any person just starting out in their photography career is to stake out their first location but to leave their camera in the car. While this may seem strange it is nonetheless important because of it because the whole point of it is for the photographer to "see" the landscapes around them as a particular scene in their photograph. While you are out staking your location, continuously ask yourself questions and observe the area around you to ensure it is exactly what you are looking for.

A couple of questions that you should ask yourself include:

1. Could I stand there and still fit the sand castle into the frame?

2. If I lower the perspective of the camera, would the picture have a more pleasing angle?

3. What direction should my subject stand?

4. Is there enough light here? Or will I need to bring artificial light?

The whole point of observation is that you need to find the answers to the questions that you ask yourself. In order to find these answers you will need to make a habit of observing the location and things around you. The more you do it, the faster you will begin to notice little things that you pass by and the more frequently you begin to look at your surroundings differently. You will also begin to notice how you can make a picture pretty much out of anything whether it is a street you are driving through or sign that you pass on the way to meet a friend.

If you are the type of person who is unable to visualize a picture before they take it, I'm sorry to say you will never become the great photographer that you want to be. However, it is not uncommon for you to feel a block every now and then and it is something that even happens to the best of photographers. The key to not breaking at these difficult moments in your career is to persevere right through them and keep observing your surrounding with a practiced eye and to have a lot of patience during this time. Once you recognize you are facing a block, it becomes your job to get passed it as best as you can and do whatever it takes to re-spark your imagination.

There are many photographers out there today and there is more than enough room for more to appear. There is no limit in the world to how many photographers can exist. A Photographer is a person who simply takes a picture. It does not matter what their skill level is nor how many years of experience they may have. It all comes down to their passion for the craft and what they are willing to do to take that perfect picture. You need to remember that a great photographer is not someone who is rich and famous because of the pictures they take, nor is it what kind of equipment they are using to take their pictures. What makes great photographers is what kind of goals they have set for themselves and whether or not they have achieved those goals in their career. A great photographer is someone who has taken the various pictures that they deem to be perfect and have done so countless times without once deviating from the path they have set for themselves.

You have the power to become this kind of photographer as well. The key is to be patient, have perseverance and to observe your surroundings because only then will you be happy with the pictures you have taken and only then will you begin to feel like a great photographer.

Chapter Two: The Basics of Your Camera and What You Need To Know About Them

So in order for you to become the great photographer that you want to become the very first thing that you need to learn is about your camera and all the parts that come along with it. With all of the available cameras out there in the market today, figuring out what kind of camera and specifications you need can be a daunting task. In this chapter I'm going to teach you everything that you need to know about how your camera works so that you can make some sense of what it means to choose a certain camera.

The Parts of Your Camera

You may be surprised to find that your camera is made up of many parts. However, there are a few parts on your camera that are more important than others and in this sections we will go through those parts in greater detail so you can understand their importance in the long run.

1. The Body Of Your Camera-this main section of your camera is the part that actually houses the important mechanics of your camera. While it may not have a important effect on the quality of the pictures that you take, it does affect how comfortable and easy it is to hold your camera.

2. The Camera Lens-this pieces is commonly referred to as the eye of your camera and it is more complex than you would believe. Every kind of different lens available today can provide a varying degree of different features to your pictures and it is important for you to know the differences between all of the lenses out there.

3. Your Camera Sensor-this piece is commonly referred to as the digital form of your film. The way that this part of your camera works is by capturing the light that comes through the camera lens and records the amount of exposure it contains. This exposure is than saved to an SD card and hence you have your picture.

4. Your Flash Card-this important piece of equipment is where all of the pictures you have taken will be saved for you to access later. This object is something that many people don't often think about when they first purchase a camera and they should. You will need to consider various things when purchasing the best kind of flash card that will best fit your needs such as it read and write speeds and how much storage it contains.

5. Your Camera's Battery-this part of your camera matters the most especially if you need your camera to last you for a certain amount of hours. This is one of the few parts of a camera that many people understand the importance of and is one that most people tend to focus on the most.

The Body of Your Camera

The overall body design of your camera will ultimately affect how you use it in your photography career. The very first thing that you will need to figure out is what kind of size camera body you will want. This can impact how comfortable it is to hold in your hand and whether or not you are going to be able to use it properly. If you have rather large hands than I recommend that you purchase a rather large camera body and if you have small hands purchase a camera with a smaller body. When you go out and buy your new camera try holding the different kinds of cameras you see until you have one that is both comfortable to hold and easy to use for your hand size.

The size of your camera is also very important to consider when purchasing a camera. You will need to be able to touch all of the necessary buttons upon your camera without fumbling it round too much. You need to keep in mind that the overall positioning on small cameras that mainly focus on point-and-shoot are cameras that are fairly simple to use. However, when you get into using smaller DSLR cameras such as the Canon's Rebel series cameras, this will be a completely different situation. You will be given extra space that your hands will need to have to spread over in order to press all of the buttons that you may have to. Again it is key to test out the camera before purchasing it so you can get an idea for yourself how comfortable and easy it is going to be to use. If the camera feels uncomfortable and awkward in your hands, simply do not get it regardless of how badly you want it. You need to remember that your comfort and ability to use it is more important than its brand name.

While every camera out there may seem similar to one another, it is important for you to remember that is not necessarily the case. You may have a general idea of what kind of capabilities a camera has without using it, but in order to find the perfect camera body for yourself you are going to need to hold it and test it out for yourself beforehand.

The Camera Lens

It is common knowledge that they are certain types of lenses that are perfect for certain situations that you find yourself filming and it is important for you to learn what these kind of difference are between camera lenses. The very first difference that you need to learn about is the difference between a zoom lens and a prime lens. A zoom lens as you probably have guessed allows you to zoom in and out on your subject. These lenses tend to be on the more expensive side and they tend to be slightly heavier and larger than most lenses you are probably used to seeing.

A Prime lens is a lens that does not give you the ability to zoom in on your subject.. These lenses are much cheaper than a zoom lens and they are much lighter and smaller to handle. The rule of thumb to follow here is that a prime lens is able to get you the sharper images that you may have been wanting than any zoom lens can and they will do just as good for your pictures than any other lens will.

The next difference that you need to learn about is the difference between a wide-angle lens, an ultra-telephoto lens, a medium lens and a standard lens. You need to keep in mind that these terms are all based upon a lens' specific focal length. A lens' focal length is measured in millimeters. However, you can think of it as a measurement of magnification. A low number means that you are zoomed out pretty far while a high number means that you are zoomed into your subject pretty close up.

1. Wide Angle Lens-these types of lenses tend to have the specific focal length measurement of 35 millimeters. It is a lens that is not quite wide and it is one that you can use to capture various things around your subject. These lenses also tend to distort the space around your subject which can increase the pictures depth and make it seem more spherical. Whether or not you want this kind of effect, it will ultimately depend on the circumstances of the picture you are taking. There are some wide-angle lenses out there available today that come with technology embedded into it that will automatically fix this distortion but those types of lenses tend to be more on the expensive side and may not be something you are willing to invest in.

2. A Standard Lens-these lenses tend to be around 35-50 millimeters in focal length and are the kind of lenses that easily capture what it is the human eye can see. These lenses tend to capture the most realistic looking pictures without any hint of distortion. These lenses are more on the affordable side and come with a standard level of quality that will still make the pictures you take look extremely professional. However, it is important to note that these kind of lenses tend to be useless when you need to capture something within a small space or are too far away to capture a specific moment.

3. A Medium Lens-these lenses fall into the focal length of 60-100 millimeters and are ones that you will not want to use as a prime lens unless you actually really need it.

4. A Telephoto Lens-this is the kind of lens you are going to want to use if you need to zoom into your subject from an incredibly far distance. One thing that you need to keep in mind is that a telephoto lens has the ability to magnify your subject many times over, they tend to be rather heavy to use and are most prone to motion blur if you move your camera around too much. Also, if you need to use the lens while you barely have enough light to see, this lens will not work for you.

The Sensor and CPU of Your Camera

The sensor of your camera is perhaps one of the most important components on your camera as it is the part responsible for capturing the light exposure that comes through your camera's lenses. In the end it does matter how your sensor was produced and what size it is because in the end it will ultimately affect the quality of the picture that you take.

The size of your camera's sensor is perhaps the most important thing about the sensor. As general rule most point-and-shoot cameras comes with a smaller sensor than a DSLR camera. If you have a camera that has a larger sensor, it will give your camera a better performance with the use of low light, will have greater depth control and you will be able to produce higher resolution photos with less noise than if your camera had a smaller sensor.

Many DSLR cameras commonly have a sensor size that is commonly referred to as an APS-C. This kind of sensor is less than half the size of your average 35 millimeter frame and is able to magnify your subject by 1.6 times. While this may seem great it is not so great if you have a telephoto lens or a wide angle lens as you will not be able to use them. While for many people this will not seem like a big deal, it is for those that need these lenses to capture the moments they need.

The most common way that you can see what kind of sensor you have it to actually test it and take a picture of something random. When choosing a camera make sure that you pay close attention to the megapixel rating of your sensor as this will give you a good idea of what kind of pictures you can take and the overall quality of pictures the camera will be able to produce. I highly recommend purchasing a camera with a sensor megapixel rating around 8-10 as this will be more than efficient for you and you will still be able to take the high quality pictures that you may be looking for.

Your Flash Card

The one thing that you need to keep in mind is that many flash cards available today come in a varying degree of certain sizes and come with their own individual speeds as well. The speed of your flash card is important because most cameras that are available on the market today are generally very fast. So, if you have a camera that is able to take a certain amount of images within a couple of seconds, you will need to have a flash card with a high writing speed so that it will be able to keep up with the amount of pictures that are being taken. As a general rule I tend to stick with cards that are either a class 6 or have a speed of 133 times. Those speeds to tend do well for the pictures that I take and they should be more than efficient for you.

You will also need to keep in mind whether or not your camera has the ability to take video. The reason that you want to know this is because you will need to have a flash card that will be able to handle the video as well and be able to save it for later use without becoming too full from the pictures you have taken.

Your Camera's Battery

For most people, this is the one factor that they look at the most when deciding what kind of camera to purchase. As a general rule you will need a camera that will be able to last you all day and compact enough that you can put it in your pocket if need be. Sometimes you may be able to purchase a high quality camera will a long battery life, but you may find yourself having to purchase a second battery just to be on the safe side.

So how do you find a camera with a long-lasting battery life? The key is to look at the ratings many companies use to gauge the efficiency of the batteries. These two ratings are how many pictures your camera can take or how many hours the battery will last. If you are looking at how many hours a battery will last this generally means that your camera can be actively functioning for a certain amount of time with the screen turned on. When looking at a battery that gauges its life by how many pictures it can take generally means that it can take those certain amount of pictures without you needing to use the LCD screen.

When you are purchasing a camera based on what kind of battery life it has it is important to know how long you will need your camera to last throughout the day and what you need it for. That way you can purchase a battery or two that will best fit your needs and the needs of your photo shoot.

Chapter Three: Knowing About Your Camera's Automatic and Shooting Settings

Now that you have a general idea of how your camera functions and what different parts of your camera are it is time that you learn about how the different setting on your camera functions. In this chapter I will teach you everything that you need to know about what kind of automatic settings your camera has and what are the different shooting modes that your cameras offers. The reason I want to teach you these basics is so that you can use your camera to its full ability and give yourself the opportunity to take all of the pictures you want without having to make it into a complicated process.

Your Camera's Different Shooting Modes

As a general rule many cameras come with their own unique set of shooting modes and they can range from being completely automatic to being completely manual. In this section I am going to point of the various shooting modes that are most commonly seen on your standard professional camera and to teach you what each setting is capable of so you know how to use it when you need to.

1. The Automatic Setting-the way that you can tell if this setting is on your camera is that it is defined by a large letter a symbol surrounded by a black box. This setting allows your camera to do all of the hard work for you such as zooming into your subject and tweaking the lens. All that is left for you to do is press the button and take your picture. There is really not much to explain here.

2. The Program Automatic Setting-the way that this setting works is that is sets both your shutter speed and aperture automatically so that you don't have to worry about doing it manually. However, this setting gives you control over other important settings on your camera such as the ISO which is the rating that is used to show how sensitive the camera's sensor is to the light in the shot. This symbol can be seen as a large letter P surrounded by a black box on your camera.

3. The Scene Setting-you can find this setting as a picture of two mountains surrounded by a black bow. Usually this setting is extremely helpful if you plan on taking pictures of the surrounding landscapes or of fast paced sporting events. This setting is extremely helpful if you want your camera to help you take the highest quality photos imaginable of these particular pictures.

4. The Shutter Priority Setting-you can find this setting on your camera by looking for the letter Tv surrounded by a large black bow on your camera. This particular setting allows you to program both the ISO and shutter speed manually. However, while it may do this for you it will still set your aperture setting automatically so you won't have to worry about doing it yourself. This setting can be extremely helpful especially if you are most concerned with having the perfect shutter speed for your photo. You may find this setting helpful if you need to take a picture of a fast moving object, sporting events or even dance recitals.

5. The Aperture Priority Setting-as you may have guessed this setting is used so that you can set both the ISO and aperture settings manually while your camera sets the shutter speed automatically. This setting is important if the only thing you are concerned with is the aperture. The aperture is used to give your photos more depth and has the greatest impact on how visual your photos are. The best way I can explain this is that if you want your subject to be as clear as possible yet still want the background to be a bit fuzzy, then a wide aperture is what you want to go for. A wide aperture gives your pictures more light to the point you won't even need to use a flash. I know this may seem confusing but I promise that this setting is much simpler than it seems to be. You can find this setting on your camera by looking for the symbol Av surrounded by a black box.

6. The Manual Setting-as you have probably guessed this setting allows you to set all of your important camera settings manual and is extremely helpful if you like to be control of every single aspect of what it takes to take the picture that you want. You can find this setting on your camera by looking for the letter M surrounded in a black box.

Your Camera's Different Flash Modes

Your camera will come with a varying amount of different flash modes and it is extremely important that you learn the difference between them. The reason it is important for you to know the differences between them is so that you don't accidentally use a flash for a picture that doesn't really need it.

1. The Automatic Flash Setting-as you probably have guessed the way that this setting works is by automatically setting the flash so it will go off only when your picture needs it. This happens when there is not enough light surrounding your subject and your camera will automatically use a sensor to gauge whether or not a flash is needed for the picture you are about to take. You can find this setting on your camera by looking for the letter A standing next to a lighting bolt ending in an arrow tip.

2. The Automatic Flash Setting With A Red Eye Reduction Feature-this feature works almost exactly as the automatic flash feature but the only difference is that it will attempt to reduce the amount of red eye that your subject has. I highly recommend that if you are going to be using your automatic flash setting, you may as well switch to using this setting as this will make your pictures turn out much better. You can find this setting on your camera by looking for the same symbol as indicated above but this time there will be a picture of an eye next to it.

3. Forced Flash and Fill in Setting-the way that this setting works is by firing a flash regardless if the camera deems it necessary or not. You can use this setting if you really think you may need the flash for a certain picture or whether you need a good laugh and blind all of your subjects temporarily. You will find this setting on your camera by looking for a lightning bolt picture that ends in an arrow tip.

4. The Shutter Flash Setting With Red-Eye Reduction-if you need to take a picture with the use of a low light setting, you will need to have your shutter speed reduced and your flash will need to set off repeatedly in order to compensate for this. This is where this setting can come and handy and can do so automatically so you don't have to worry about it. To find this setting look for the flash symbol and next to it there will be the letter S and a picture of an eye.

5. The No Flash Setting-as this setting entails, you can use this setting when you don't need a flash to go off. To find this setting on your camera look for the flash symbol surrounded by an X.

Your Camera's Video Mode

Most of the time when people are discussing the topic of photography, very rarely will they mention your camera's video mode. Almost every single camera on the market today offers this function and it can prove to be handy when you feel the need to videotape something of great importance. Of course with every single different type of camera out there, each camera will, have their own unique video setting.

For example, a simple point-and shoot camera will have the ability to automatically focus on your subject without you having to worry about doing so while other compact cameras may have difficulty in focusing on your subject. A DSLR camera has the ability to take the highest quality video possible; however it will have a harder time focusing on your subject unless you switch it to the manual setting where you can focus on the subject instead.

As a general rule, you can easily save the videos you take on the same flash card that your pictures are automatically saved on, but you may find some cameras that have a special folder dedicated to holding your different videos. The tricky part is finding these videos when it is time to upload them onto your computer. Always try to look for the files ending in .AVI, .MOV or. MP4 as these are common video files that end with this kind of code. You can use these files to upload onto your computer or YouTube but some cameras will require you to format the video first before you are able to upload it onto your laptop or desktop.

Knowing the different settings that your camera has to offer are extremely important. You would buy a brand new car without knowing important details such as the inside features of the car or what kind of gas mileage it gets, would you? The same can be said for a camera and it is important to know what these settings are capable of so you can use them appropriately if you find that you have to. Knowing the differences between these different settings and what they can do can set you on the path to becoming a great photographer and can help make your pictures come out as perfect as possible.

Conclusion

Knowing the basics of photography is not the most complicated thing in the world. Photography in general is a very simple career to follow and it has absolutely nothing to do with how many years of experience a person has or even what kind of high tech equipment they use. It all comes down to the kind of pictures they take and who they are as a person. You can take the most beautiful pictures out of any photographer out there, but if you have the attitude of someone who is the best at what they do, you will never become a great photographer.

There are varying basics of photography that you need to learn in order to set on a path to become the world's greatest photographer. You need to know about the different parts of your camera, what these parts means to you and your comfort level, what different settings each camera has and how they can help you to take high quality pictures. Once you have the basics down all that is left for you to do is finding something that is worthy of taking a picture, point your camera and shoot.

About Us

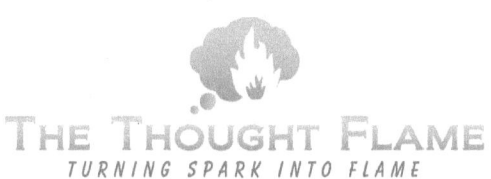

The Thought Flame is committed to add value to its customers through various books, online courses and other resources. You can learn more about us and our books at www.thethoughtflame.com.

Don't forget to check out our amazing **online video courses** at www.thethoughtflame.com/courses/ to take your knowledge to another level.

To check out our **extraordinary collection of diet/cookbooks**, visit http://www.thethoughtflame.com/category/non-fictional/cookbooks/ .

As a part of our valued relationship with our customers, we keep providing you free promotional books, courses and other stuff on subscribing with us on our site. We have a strict anti-spam policy and assure you no spam mails will be sent to your mailbox.

To subscribe with us, visit www.thethoughtflame.com.

Like our work and would like to say thanks?

Buy us a cup of coffee at www.thethoughtflame.com/coffee/

Author

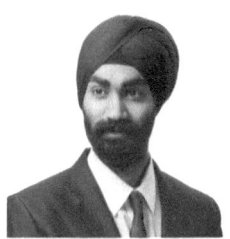

Amarpreet Singh is an avid learner and his passion for education has made him travel, work and study all across the world. He holds three masters degrees, including MBA, from top universities in Asia.

He is author of dozens of books, many of which are Amazon's bestseller, varying in various topics and categories. He also teaches many online courses having thousands of students across the world.

He has a keen interest in international affairs, economics, global poverty and politics, financial markets and entrepreneurship, and strives to be part of a community that shares the same passion.

He has worked as consultant with organizations like Airbus and The World Bank.

He loves travelling and learning about new cultures, and has been fortunate to live/work/travel/study in countries like India, China, Korea, US, South Africa, Japan, Philippines, Singapore, Canada etc., and learn about the culture and lifestyle in each of them.

To check out more of his work, visit www.thethoughtflame.com